FlipSigns

Michael Jenner

Prestel Munich · London · New York

Library of Congress Control Number: 2001092039

Prestel books are available worldwide. Please contact
your nearest bookseller or any of the addresses below
for information concerning your local distributor.

Prestel Verlag
Mandlstrasse 26
D-80802 Munich
Germany
Tel.: (89) 38-17-09-0
Fax.: (89) 38-17-09-35
www.prestel.de

4 Bloomsbury Place
London
WC1A 2QA
Tel.: (020) 7323 5004
Fax.: (020) 7636 8004

175 Fifth Avenue, Suite 402
New York
NY 10010
Tel.: (212) 995 2720
Fax.: (212) 995 2733
www.prestel.com

Editorial direction: Philippa Hurd
Design: Matthias Hauer, Gunta Lauck (ass.)
Typeface: T&T Form by Bernd Möllenstädt
Image Editing: phg, Martinsried
Printing and binding: Graspo, Zlín
Printed in the Czech Republic

ISBN 3-7913-2584-1

FlipSigns

Contents

16–17

18–19

20–21

22–23

24–25

26–27

28–29

30–31

32–33

34–37

38–39

40–41

42–43

44–45

46–47

48–49

50–51

52–53

54–55

56–57

58–59

60–61

62–63

64–65

66–67

68–69

70–71

72–73

74–75

76–77

78–79

80–81

82–83

84–85

86–87

88–89

90–91

92–93

94–95

96–97

98–99

100–101

102–103

104–105

106–107

108–109

110–111

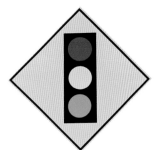

112–113

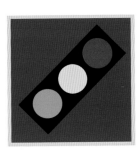

114–115

116–117

118–119

120–121

122–125

DEAD
END

126–127

128–129

130–131

132–133

134–135

136–139

140–143

Introduction

Wherever we turn in the modern world signs of all shapes and sizes confront us. Some are so new and baffling we can't easily decipher them, while others appear so old, familiar and somehow so self-evident that they have simply slipped into our subconscious and we are no longer properly aware of them. Either way, we barely pause to give most signs a second glance as we progress on our erratic journeys through the urban and automotive jungle.

I'm not sure exactly when I first took serious note of the amazing visual subtext of meaning and symbolism lurking in road signs. But if my photographic record is anything to go by then my eyes were opened about twenty-five years ago in Italy, for it was then and there I started taking pictures of signage of various types. Perhaps the distinctly different Italian graphic style attracted my attention. For what had become virtually invisible at home through long exposure as an everyday icon suddenly looked refreshingly different.

Prominent among these was a sign showing a man crossing the street. His angular form and stylish pose seemed so in keeping with the natural elegance of real-life Italians strutting their stuff on the piazza that I couldn't resist documenting him as an eloquent emblem of the national character. The alert form of this pedestrian also suggested a degree of urgency, which seemed quite understandable given the hectic tempo of Italian traffic. At any rate, quite out of the blue, a simple street sign had conveyed something way beyond its intended function. In a sense, a mute figure had come to life.

After that the genie was out of the bottle. Street signs had begun to talk and I was tuned in to their mysterious language. Wherever I went I could never ignore their silent but insistent claims on my attention. Even the most simplistic, pared down matchstick man became as intriguing as a miniature masterpiece in an art gallery. In fact, the more drained of humanity the figures became the more they seemed to have something important to say about the basic contradictions of the human condition. For, in spite of our glorious individuality, what are we ultimately when reduced to bare essentials but an assemblage of two arms, two legs, a torso and a head? That is surely how we must look when simplified to the limit. The truth is: signs are us.

So the sign folk (as I came to know them) communicated a message of sorts in their blunt no-nonsense fashion, and it was all the more powerful because these figures were not designed to have any meaning beyond their specific function. Indeed, the power of their mute communication was actually intensified by its non-verbal nature. Like mime artists they spoke a global language of silent gesture. As such, they were the embodiment of universality, archetypal figures that transcended all frontiers of race and culture. And that was completely in keeping with their intended role, for what else should one expect of a universal symbol but precisely that?

Even so, the simple identikit figures and faceless symbols of street signs that came off the industrial conveyor belt still did not provide the most obvious vehicle for creative expression. They looked so entirely sufficient unto themselves. It surely couldn't matter less to them whether they were heeded or ignored. It was other people who drew up and enforced the rules and instructions that they personified. So what was there for me to do but just record them? Accordingly, for several years all I could do was to photograph signs here and there on my travels and archive them like a collector of stamps or butterflies.

In the process I came to appreciate the many subtle differences that could distinguish, for example, one matchstick man from another. I reckoned there must be a common ancestor from whom all subsequent variations were descended. It dawned on me that the scratched figures on the walls of caves must be the ultimate point of origin, leading from there via other prehistoric carvings and more sophisticated versions on Egyptian obelisks and Babylonian friezes. And so the mass-produced, machine-like figures of the present day had a lineage every bit as noble as the human beings they represented. Furthermore, the physical outlines of people portrayed on modern road signs would be instantly recognizable to those who had lived thousands of years ago.

As things proceeded, I became fascinated by the more complex type of warning signs, particularly those alerting the observer to some kind of imminent danger: from the almost comic scenario of a man taking a tumble on a slippery surface or putting a foot through a fragile roof to the more sinister, life-threatening situation that showed a limp human form lying on his back with a black thunderbolt of high voltage electricity hovering overhead. In this way a disturbing world of mortal threats and hidden menaces was revealed.

It was also amazing to discover some unexpectedly sentimental touches, say in the lively bounce of children scampering arm in arm as portrayed on a school playground sign, or in the fragile stoop of elderly people tenderly supporting one another across the road outside an old folk's home. With that came the realization that the sign folk could relate to one another. All of human life was there. I was accumulating a cast of characters expressing various states of being that offered huge potential for a much bigger, as yet unscripted spectacle.

Other things were also making themselves felt. Dramatic motifs such as brutal red diagonal lines slicing through defenceless figures exuded a distinct threat of violence. Signs forbidding one kind of activity or another all shared the common currency of this thick red line that demanded respect and obedience. Meanwhile, on a purely visual level, stark color combinations – most usually red and black on white or black on yellow – made a compelling graphic impact as if some abstract geometric art was struggling to get out.

But still, as a photographer, all I could do was to go on recording. It was not until I learned the basic techniques of digital image manipulation that something new started to happen. Only then did I realize that my private collection of sign folk could now emerge from their sign world onto a canvas of my own making. Removed from their frames the figures immediately became something else. It was like seeing paintings in a picture gallery step out of their frames and take up an independent existence. Viewed in isolation, outside their context, the sign folk entered another dimension entirely. Stripped of their given meaning they may have been, but how eloquent these anonymous figures with their frozen postures and blank features now appeared. They threw down a challenge to the onlooker to seek various meanings where previously there had only been one simple message or diktat.

On my computer screen I could line them up in serried rank-and-file or arrange them like pieces of Lego. These small figures were perhaps insignificant

on their own, but when amassed in numbers they flowed in a great river of humanity as portrayed in those hopelessly idealized visions of the socialist paradise: the power of the people celebrated in the epic quality of the everyday. Something else happened when an individual figure was magnified. It achieved a kind of monumental status like a super-being, heroic and eternal. Meanwhile, there was always an element of the comic strip about these curiously stylized creations that reduced the human to a simplistic Pop-art sketch. And behind it all there lurked the distinct impression of a story being told. Instinctively, I groped to seize the threads of a narrative as elusive and intriguing as ancient hieroglyphs.

Flipped this way and that, out of context, the figures might appear caught in a chaotic collective dance of contrary intentions. Dramatic changes occurred with every twist of the kaleidoscope. A man lying inert on his back when flipped vertically was miraculously transformed into a dynamic figure like an acrobat in mid-somersault. Man slipping over suddenly became man flying. Falling down and taking off were now revealed as two sides of the same coin. And beyond the individual figures a complex abstract pattern replicated itself in an endless chain of movement in which all contradictory movements were ultimately cancelled out in a much bigger pattern.

Meanwhile, the abstract symbols of black arrows and red lines with their powerful geometry were asking to be turned into complex patterns where the original element soon submerged into a grander design. It was at this point I became aware that in order to achieve a stronger graphic effect it was necessary to get as far away as possible from the original photograph of the real-life sign that had begun the process. That meant removing all evidence of the sign in situ. Telltale traces of weathering and other blemishes such as dents, scratches and rust that looked so authentic as documentary realism were replaced by a smooth expanse of pristine color. They now appeared crisp and fresh just as they must have looked on the drawing board before they went into service as signs: pure flights of creative fancy.

Something curious also happened with words. When flipped and spun into patterns even simple messages and monosyllabic commands such as STOP and DO NOT ENTER, obvious and harmless enough in their own context, acquired a

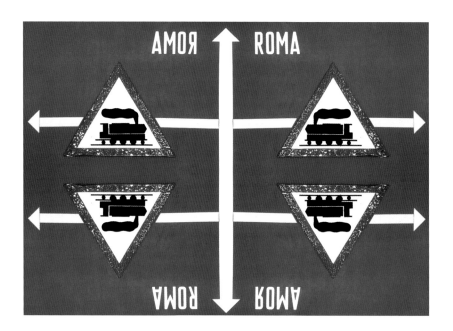

verbal opacity not without mystery and occasionally menace. DANGER, DEAD
END, NO OUTLET. An endless maze of Kafkaesque proportions loomed.

The order of this book follows broadly my own experience and experi-
ments with signage. The introduction is illustrated with some examples from
my early Italian collection. In addition to the stylish pedestrian already de-
scribed are two road signs of a now defunct genre that are rather appealing in
their worn and weathered state. One offers the two cities of Venezia and
Ravenna like a stark existential choice with no clue given as to which fork
might be the major road. Another shows the main road leading only to Roma
with an ancient steam locomotive crossing on a minor side road. When I first
flipped this sign I discovered that ROMA spelled backwards gives AMOR. Deli-
cious. Also featured here is another firm favorite still in its original colors: the
square-cut white figure of a man on a green background running for the emergency exit. The geometric pattern created by the rectangular arms and legs is
particularly compelling.

The main body of the book divides into three: HUMAN FIGURES, WORDS
AND SYMBOLS, COMPOSITIONS AND ABSTRACTIONS. The borderlines between

the sections may seem hazy in places, but however disparate the imagery, the unifying idea has been to pursue a series of creative graphic adventures with signage in various forms and colors, exploring the many possibilities. The emphasis throughout has been on achieving a strong result rather than making patterns for their own sake. The compositions and abstractions in the final section enter a different category, far removed from their literal starting point. But where the book ends, after all, is just an arbitrary halting place: for the unsung art of the intriguing signage that exists all around us in the public domain offers a rich source for future creativity.

FlipSigns

Schoolchildren (1)

Schoolchildren (3)

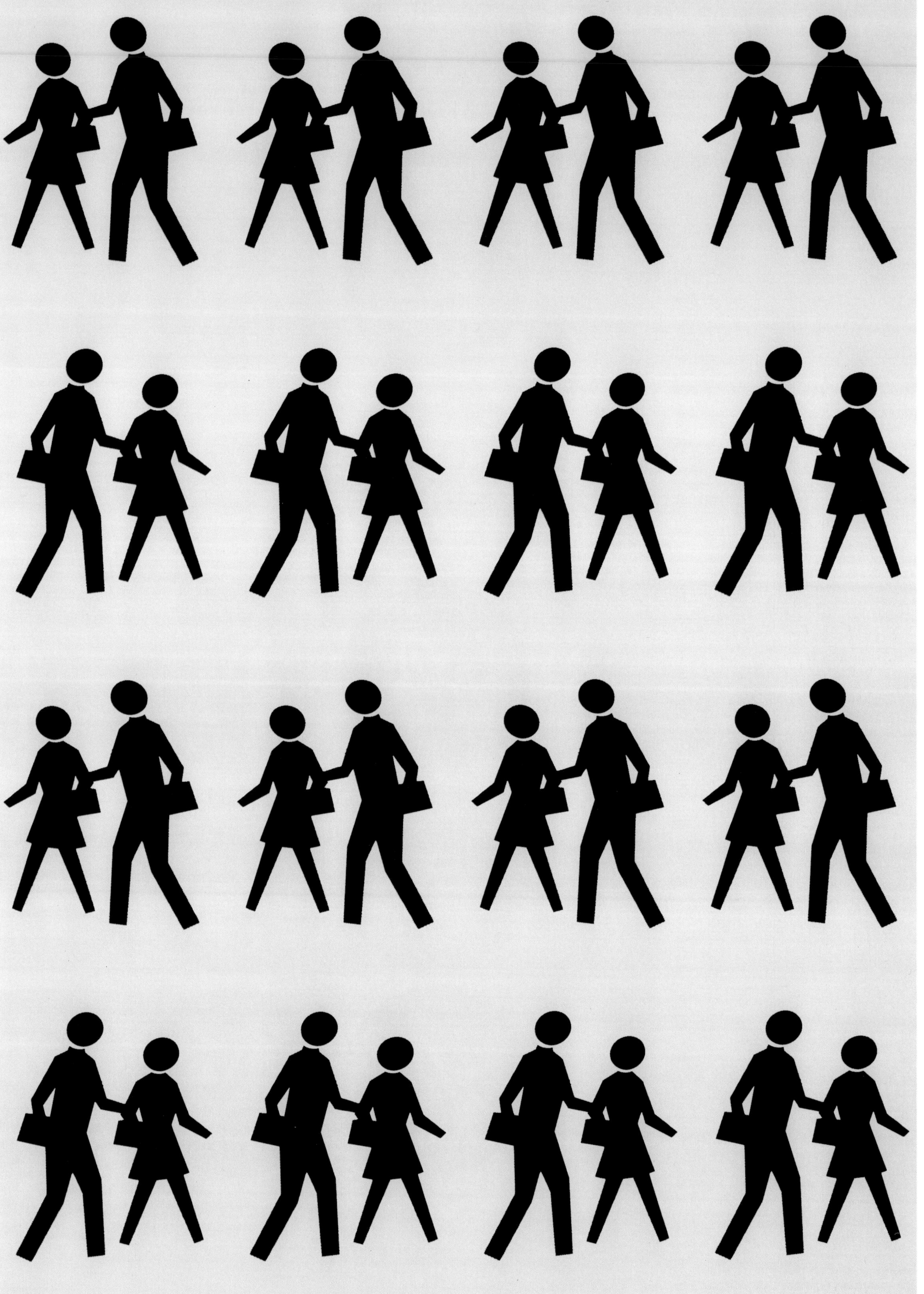

Mother and daughter

Father and daughter (1)

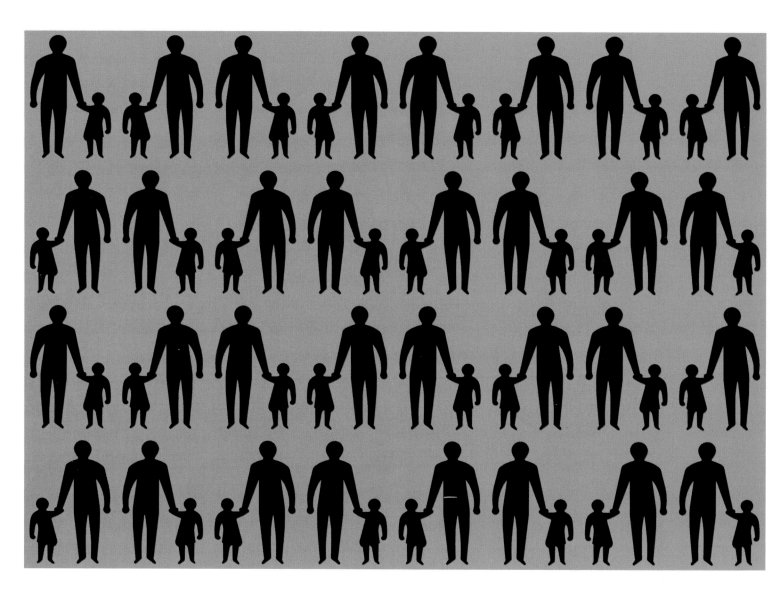

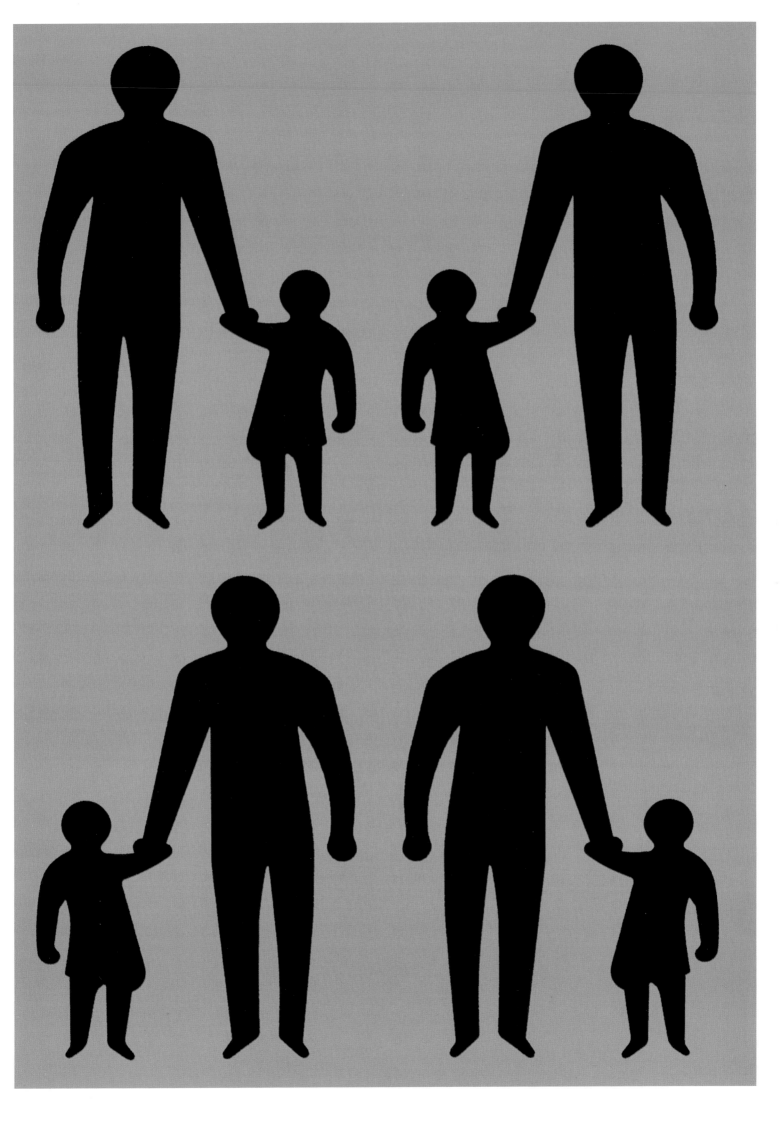

Father and daughter (2)

Slippery floor

Emergency exit

Roadworks

Reflecting figures

Rotating figures (1)

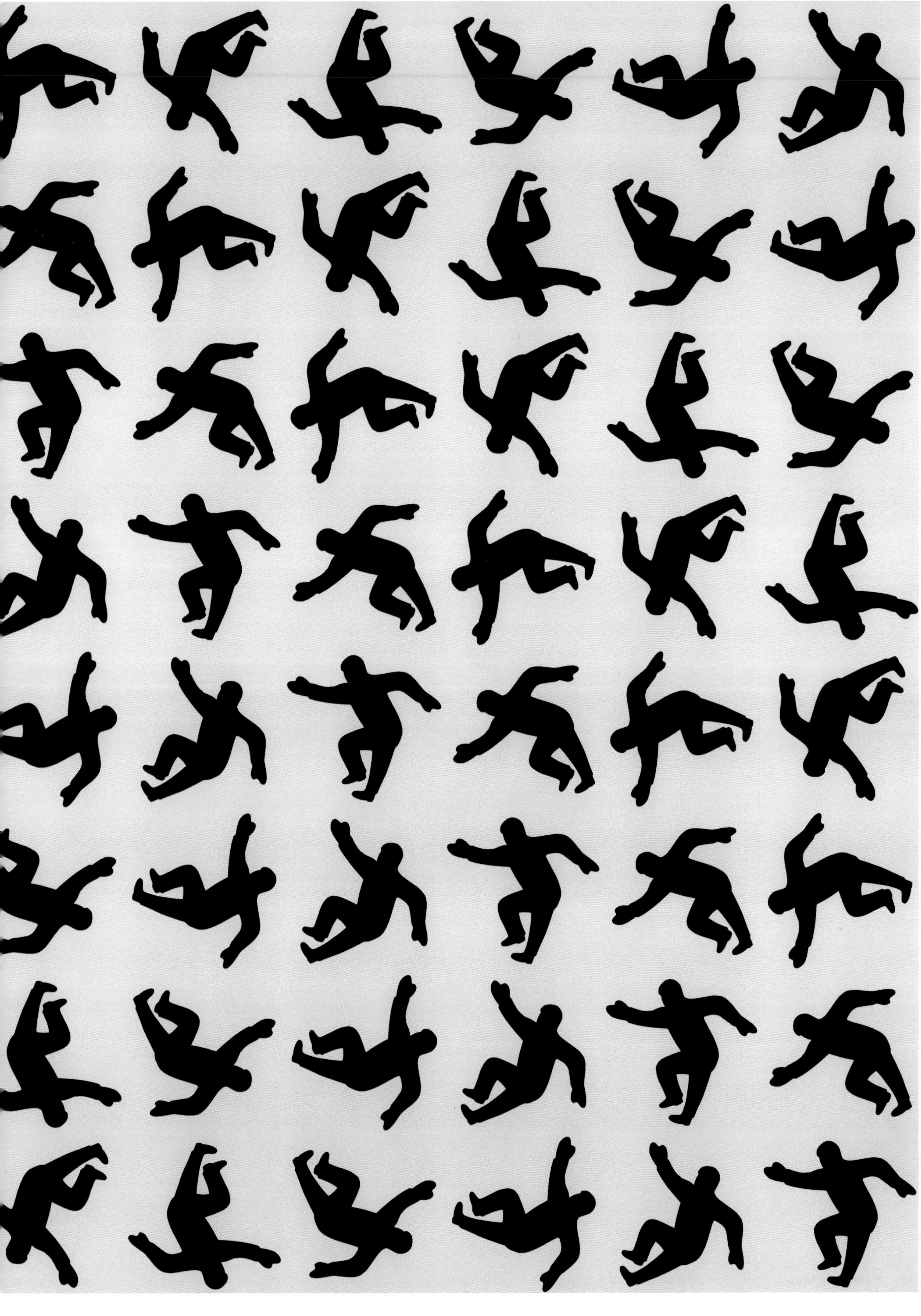

Rotating figures (2)

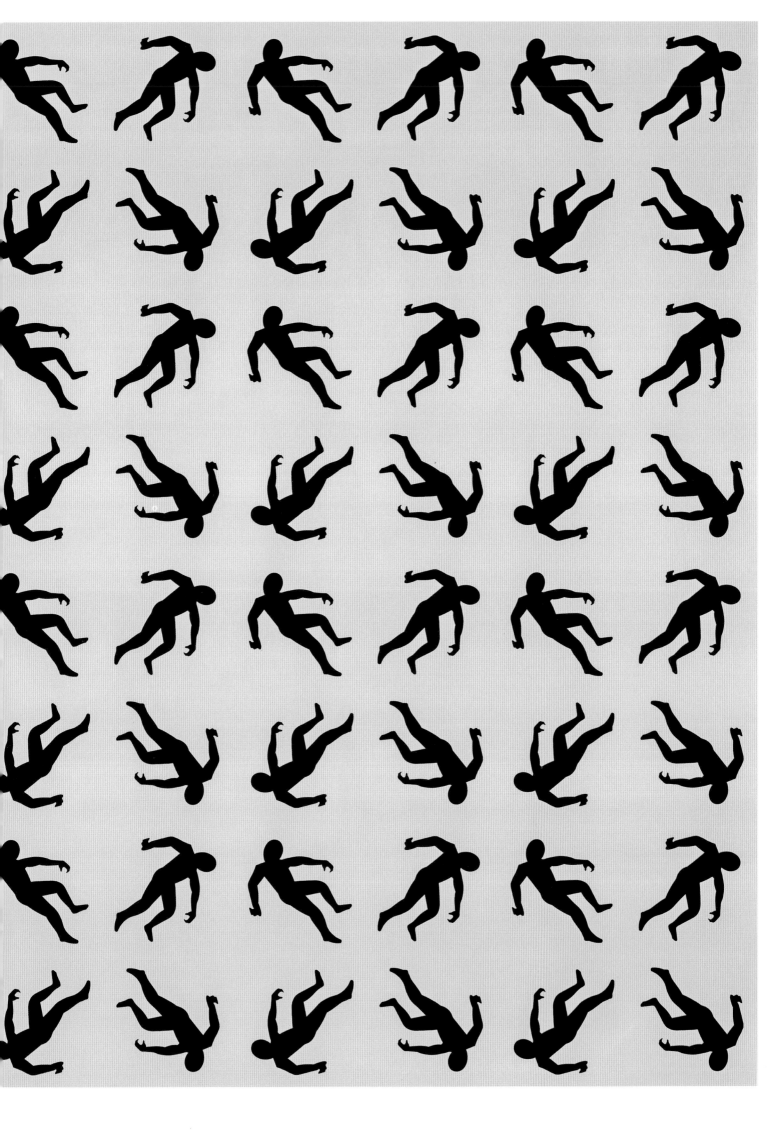

Underground blues

Floating stairs

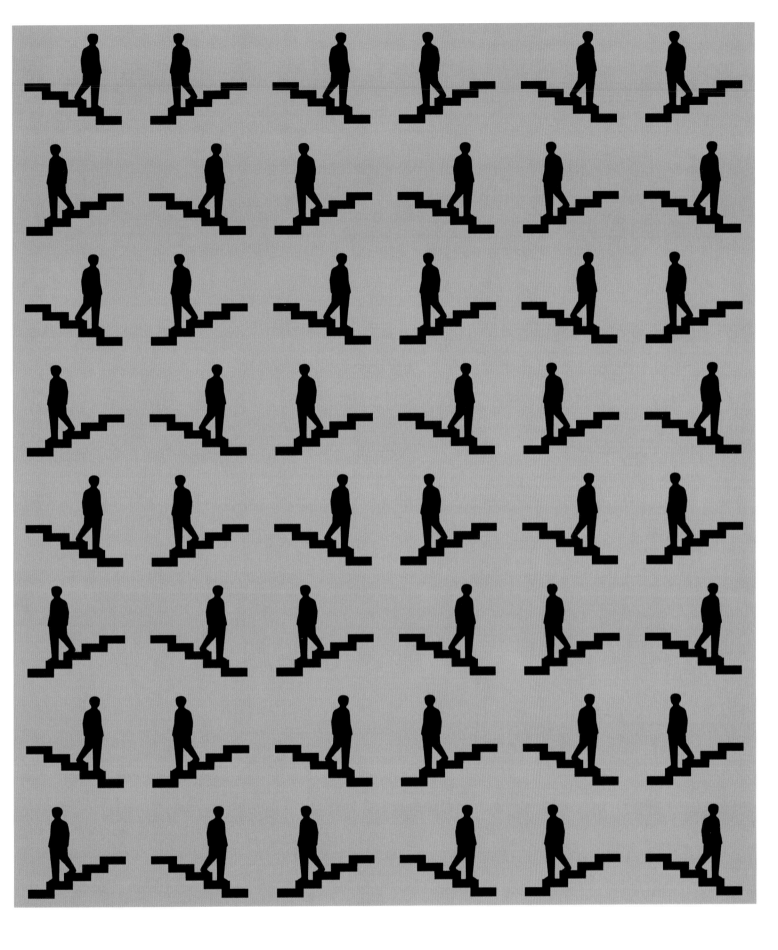

Danger: fragile roof

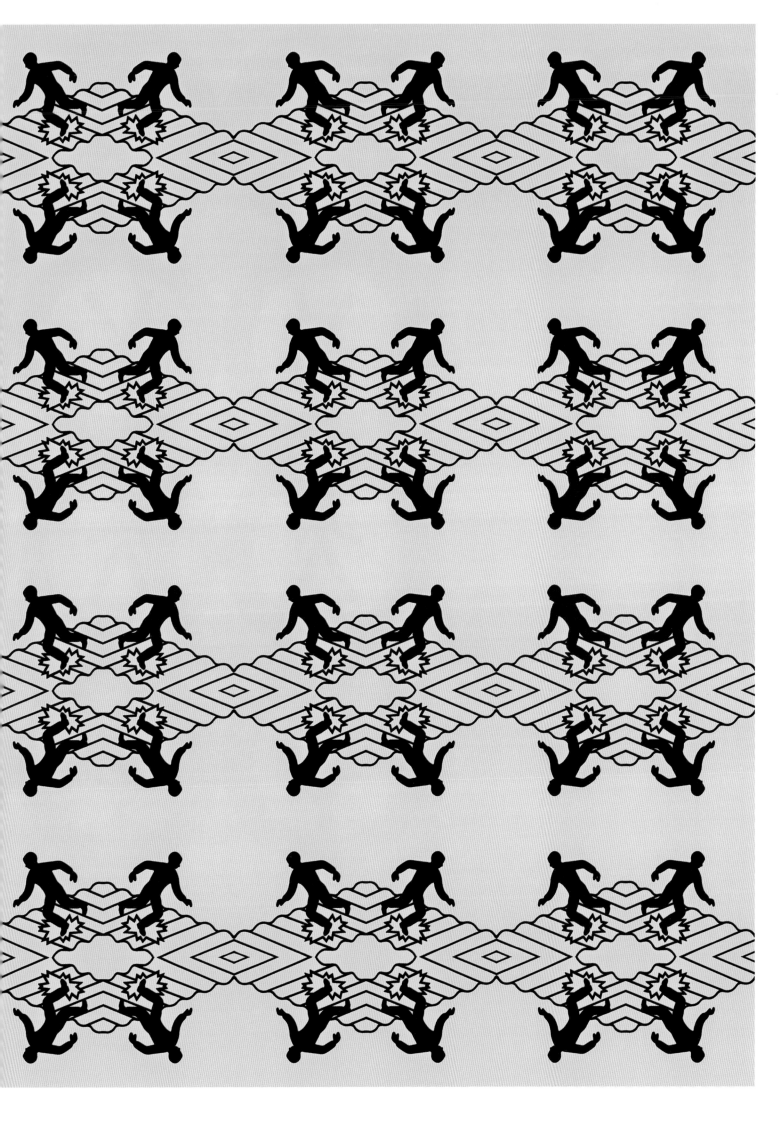

Matchstick man walking

Matchstick man: one head, four bodies.

Pedestrian crossing

Blue Order of the Pedestrian

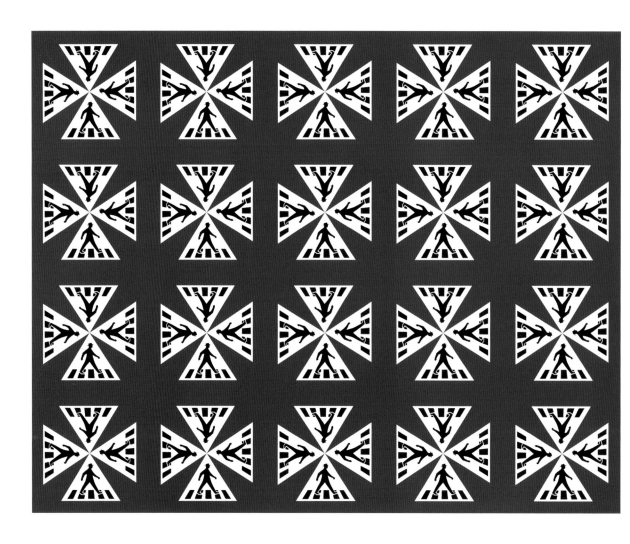

Pedestrian crossing on red

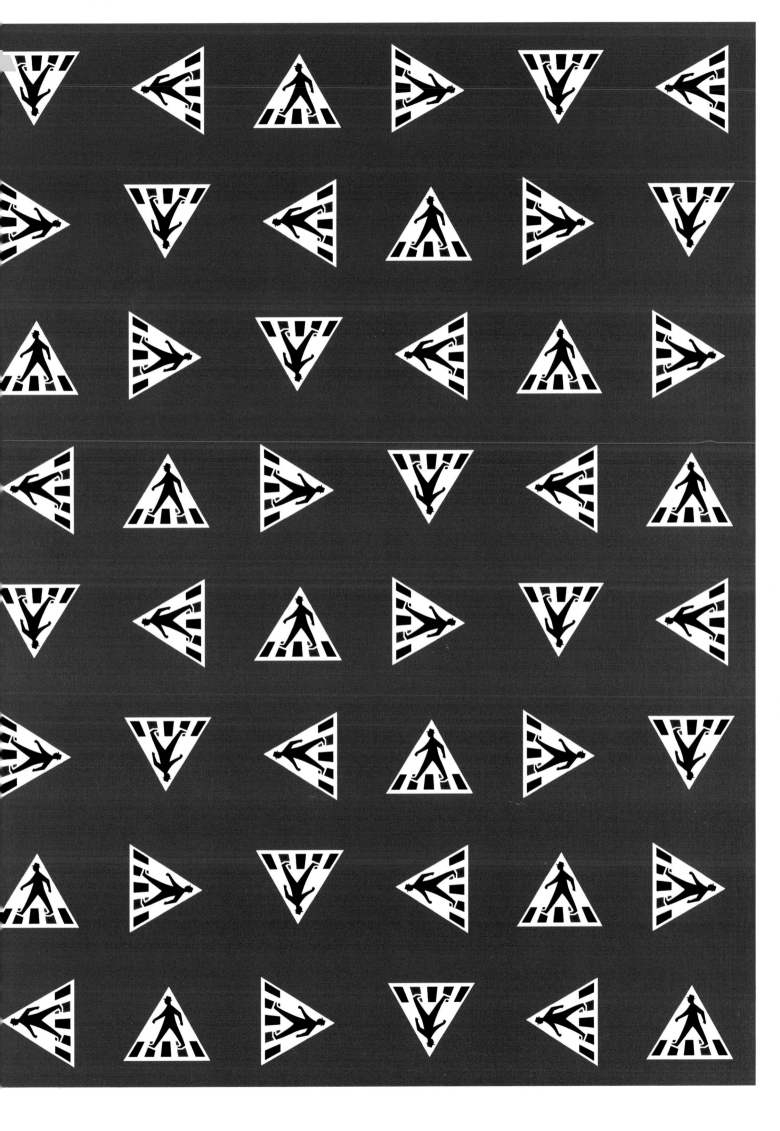

Pedestrian crossing on yellow

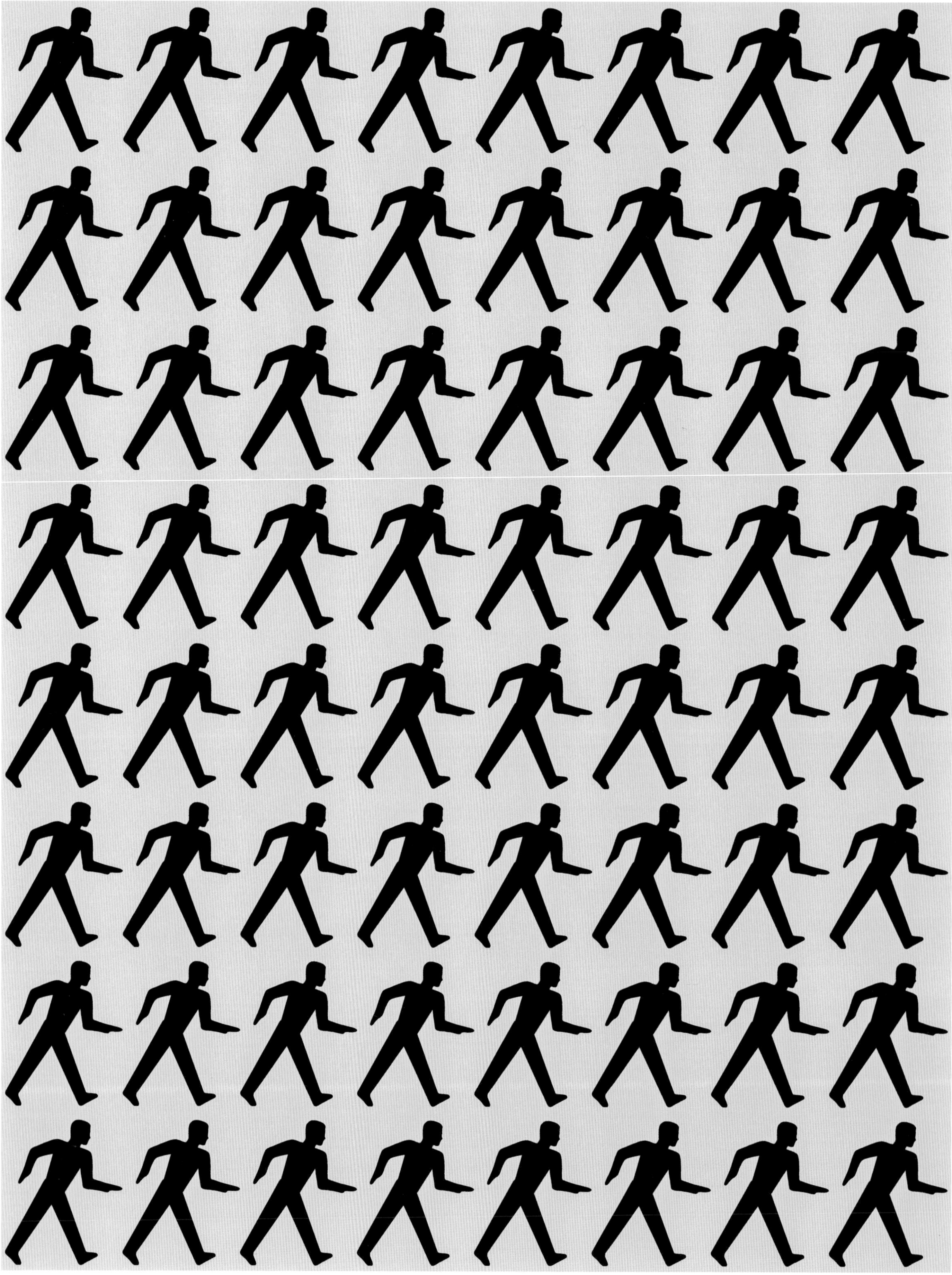

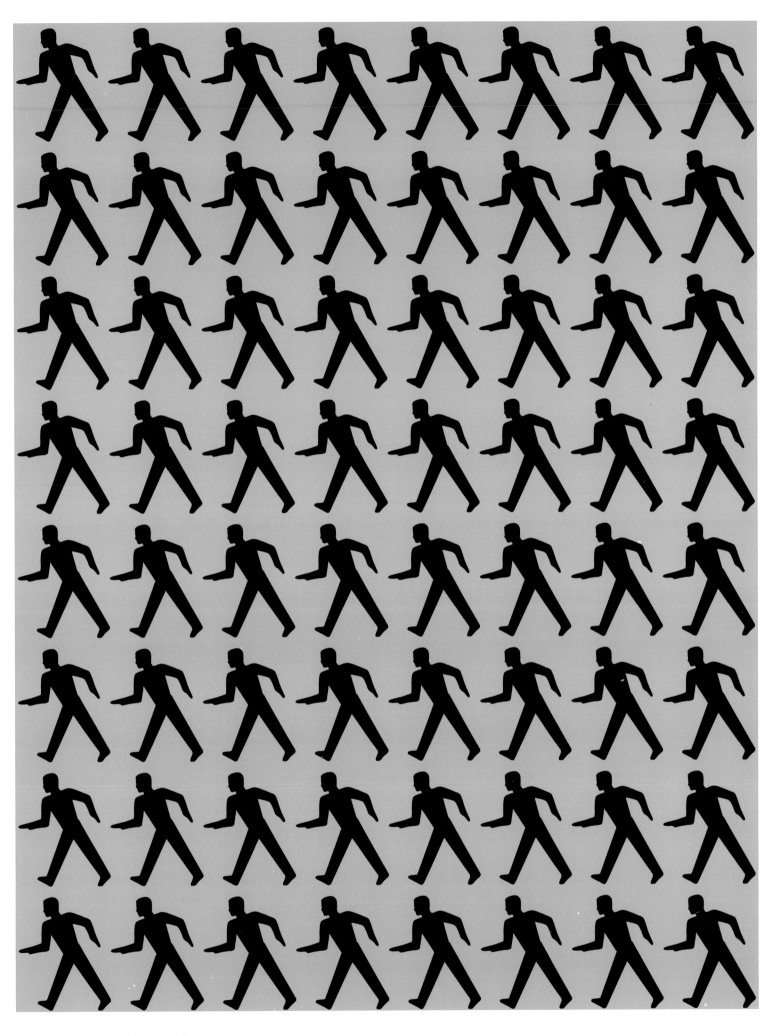

Pedestrians on the march

No entry man

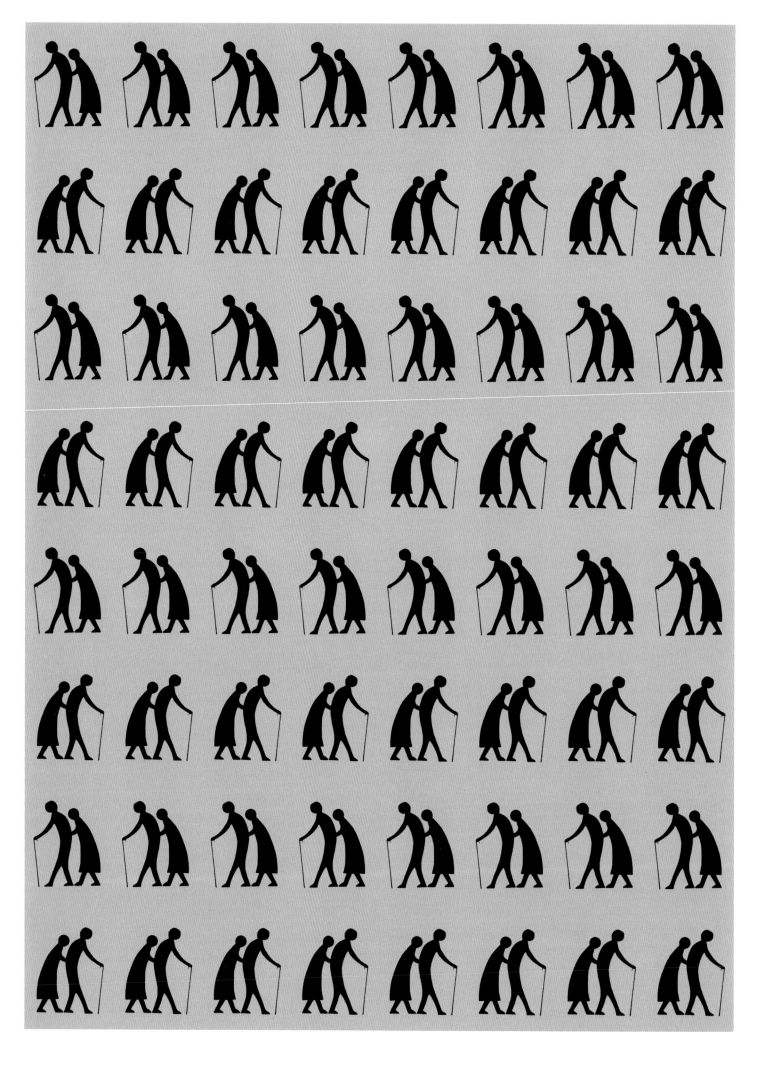

Elderly folk crossing

Keep out!

Swimming area

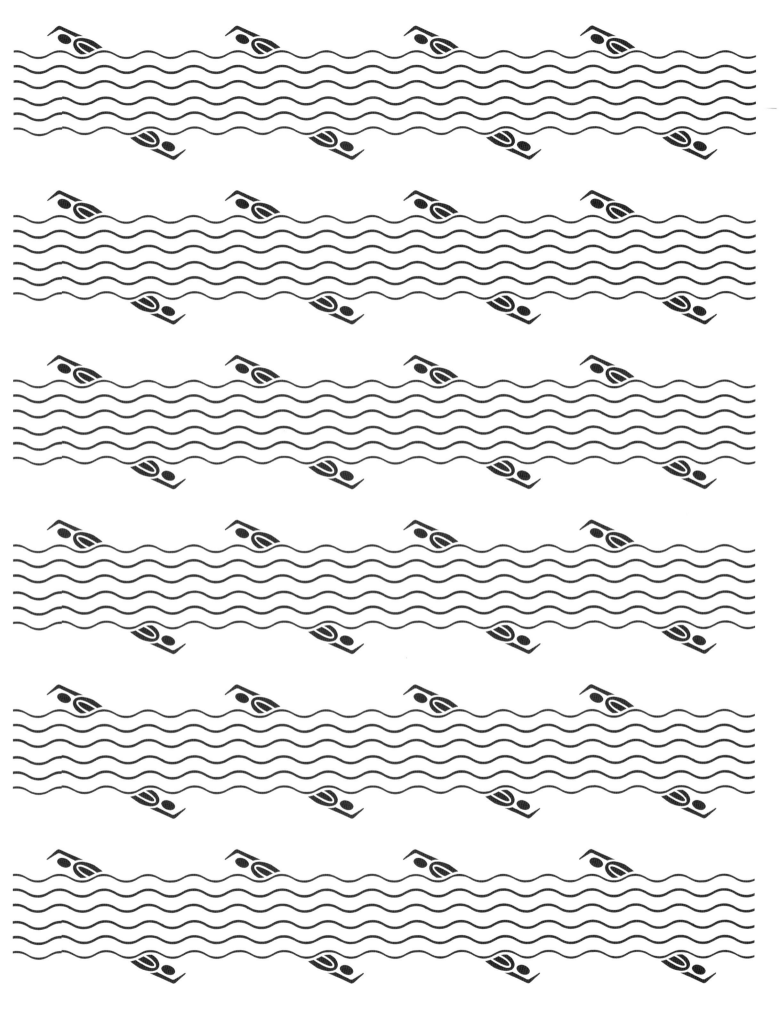

Danger of death

Tow-away zone

Rolling trucks

73

Human Figures | **Words and Symbols** | Compositions and Abstractions

Bicycle chain

Fire hose reel

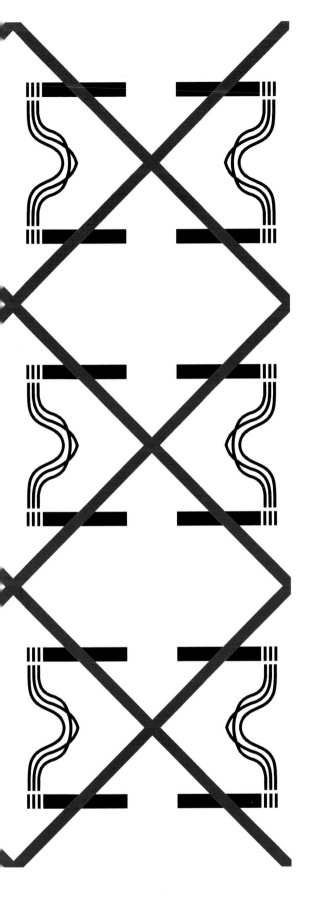

No smoking (1)

79

No smoking (2)

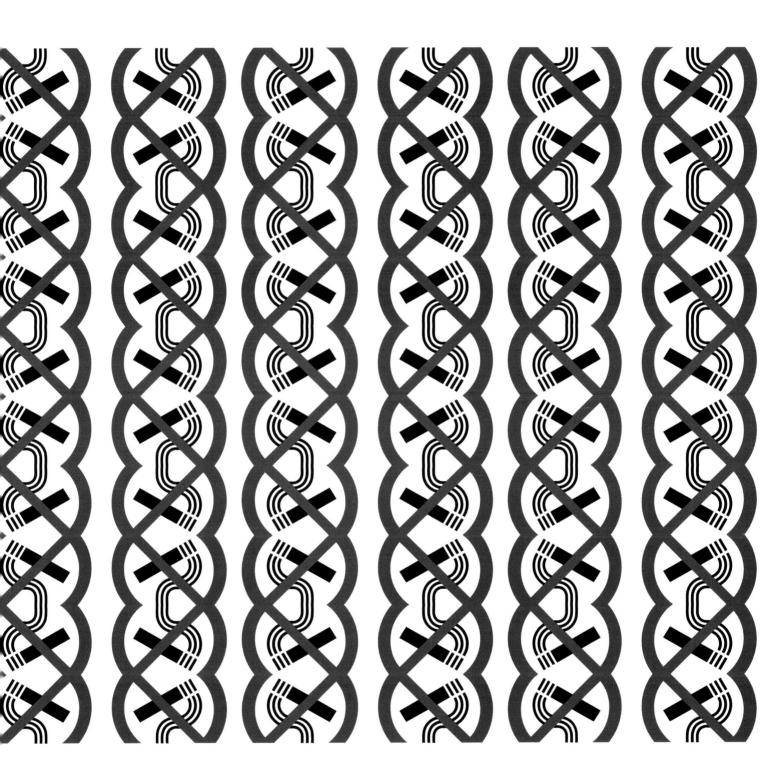

Disabled parking

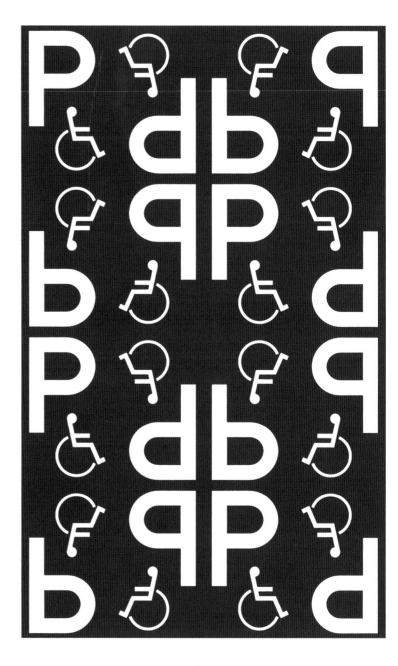

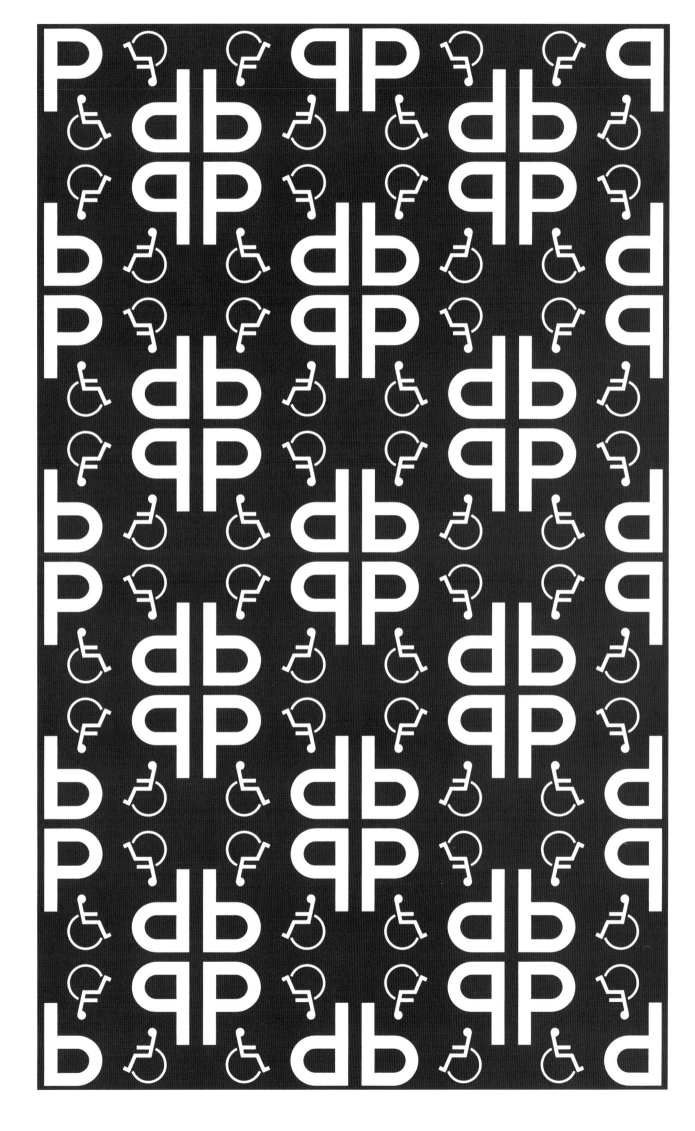

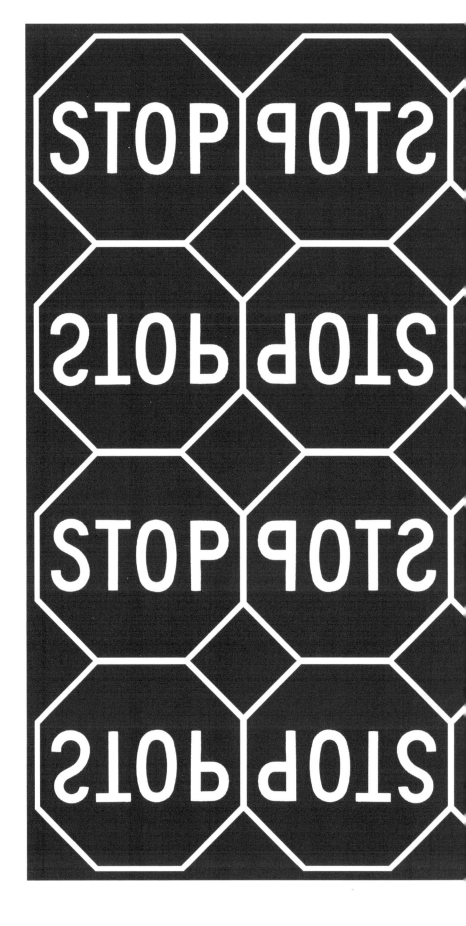

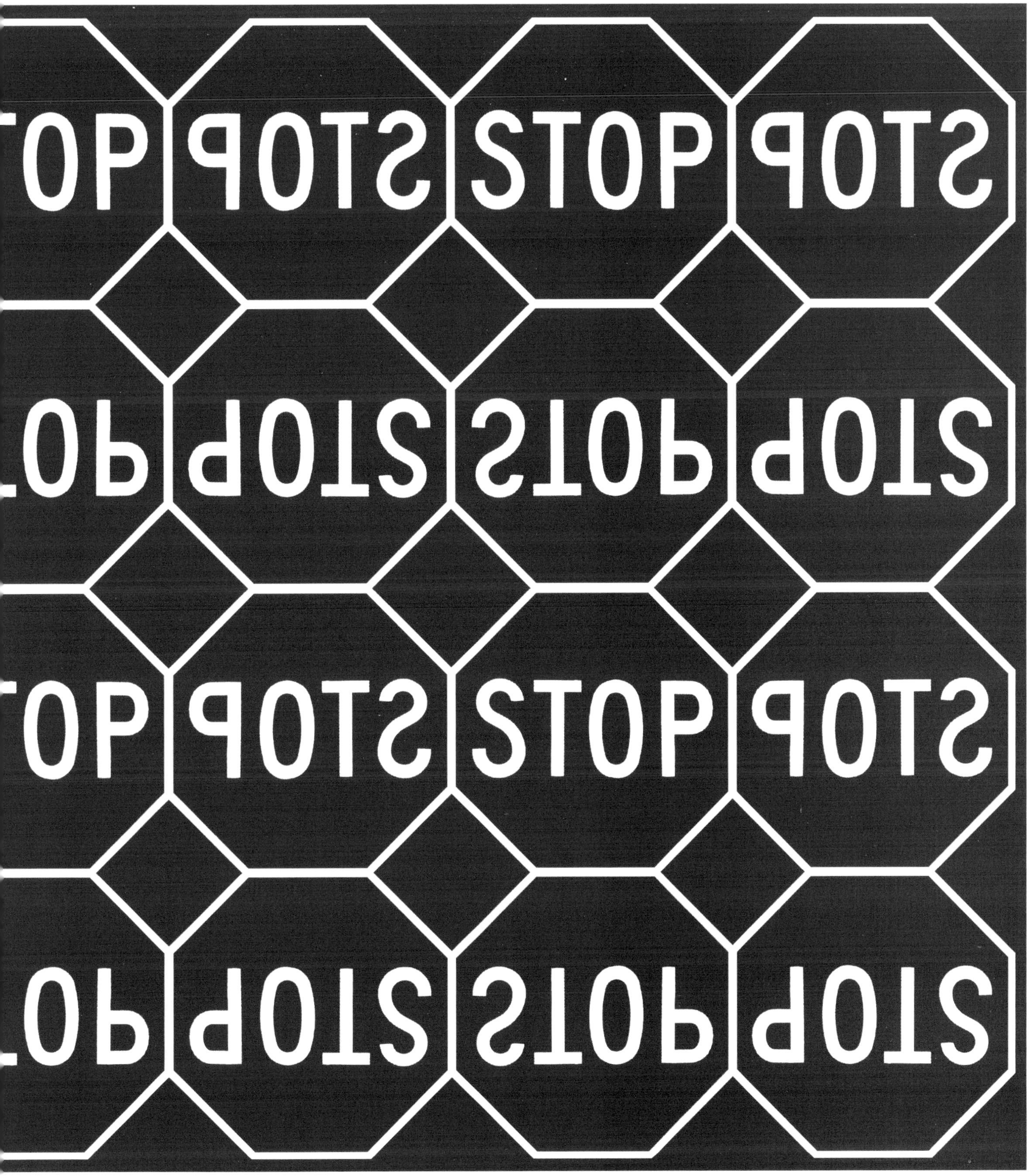
STOP
STOP

Day and Night

JOUR ЯUOႱ JOUR ЯUOႱ JOUR ЯUOႱ JOUR ЯUOႱ
ET ТƎ ET ТƎ ET ТƎ ET ТƎ
NUIT TIUИ NUIT TIUИ NUIT TIUИ NUIT TIUИ
TIUИ NUIT TIUИ NUIT TIUИ NUIT TIUИ NUIT
 TƎ ET TƎ ET TƎ ET TƎ ET
ႱOUR ЯUOႱ ႱOUR ЯUOႱ ႱOUR ЯUOႱ ႱOUR ЯUOႱ

JOUR ЯUOႱ JOUR ЯUOႱ JOUR ЯUOႱ JOUR ЯUOႱ
ET ТƎ ET ТƎ ET ТƎ ET ТƎ
NUIT TIUИ NUIT TIUИ NUIT TIUИ NUIT TIUИ
TIUИ NUIT TIUИ NUIT TIUИ NUIT TIUИ NUIT
TƎ ET TƎ ET TƎ ET TƎ ET
ႱOUR ЯUOႱ ႱOUR ЯUOႱ ႱOUR ЯUOႱ ႱOUR ЯUOႱ

JOUR ЯUOႱ JOUR ЯUOႱ JOUR ЯUOႱ JOUR ЯUOႱ
ET ТƎ ET ТƎ ET ТƎ ET ТƎ
NUIT TIUИ NUIT TIUИ NUIT TIUИ NUIT TIUИ
TIUИ NUIT TIUИ NUIT TIUИ NUIT TIUИ NUIT
TƎ ET TƎ ET TƎ ET TƎ ET
ႱOUR ЯUOႱ ႱOUR ЯUOႱ ႱOUR ЯUOႱ ႱOUR ЯUOႱ

JOUR ЯUOႱ JOUR ЯUOႱ JOUR ЯUOႱ JOUR ЯUOႱ
ET ТƎ ET ТƎ ET ТƎ ET ТƎ
NUIT TIUИ NUIT TIUИ NUIT TIUИ NUIT TIUИ
TIUИ NUIT TIUИ NUIT TIUИ NUIT TIUИ NUIT
ET ТƎ ET ТƎ ET ТƎ ET ТƎ
ЯUOႱ ႱOUR ЯUOႱ ႱOUR ЯUOႱ ႱOUR ЯUOႱ ႱOUR

WRONG
WAY

WRONG | WRONG | WRONG
WAY | WAY | WAY

WAY | WAY | WAY
WRONG | WRONG | WRONG

WRONG | WRONG | WRON
WAY | WAY | WAY

WAY | WAY | WAY
WRONG | WRONG | WRONG

WRONG | WRONG | WRON
WAY | WAY | WAY

WAY | WAY | WAY
WRONG | WRONG | WRONG

WRONG | WRONG | WRON
WAY | WAY | WAY

WAY | WAY | WAY
WRONG | WRONG | WRONG

WRONG WAY WRONG WAY WRONG WAY WRONG WAY WRONG WAY

WAY WAY WAY WAY WAY
WRONG WRONG WRONG WRONG WRONG

WRONG WAY WRONG WAY WRONG WAY WRONG WAY WRONG WAY

WAY WAY WAY WAY WAY
WRONG WRONG WRONG WRONG WRONG

WRONG WAY WRONG WAY WRONG WAY WRONG WAY WRONG WAY

WAY WAY WAY WAY WAY
WRONG WRONG WRONG WRONG WRONG

WRONG WAY WRONG WAY WRONG WAY WRONG WAY WRONG WAY

WAY WAY WAY WAY WAY
WRONG WRONG WRONG WRONG WRONG

5 miles per hour

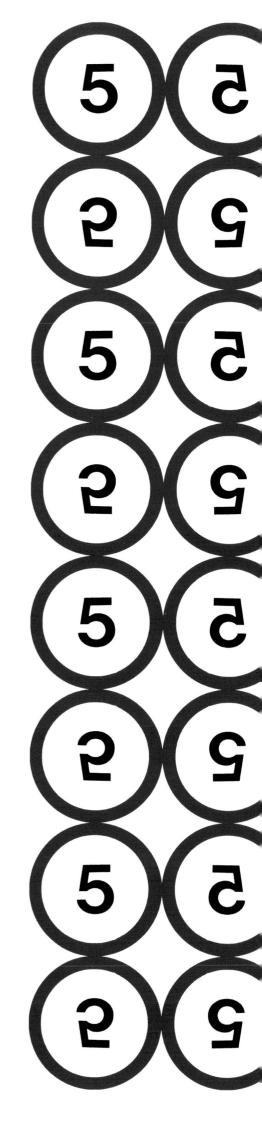

Euro

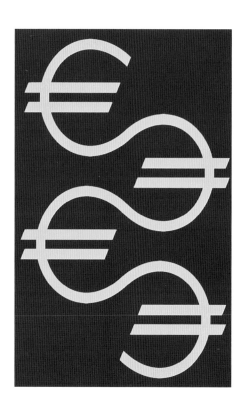

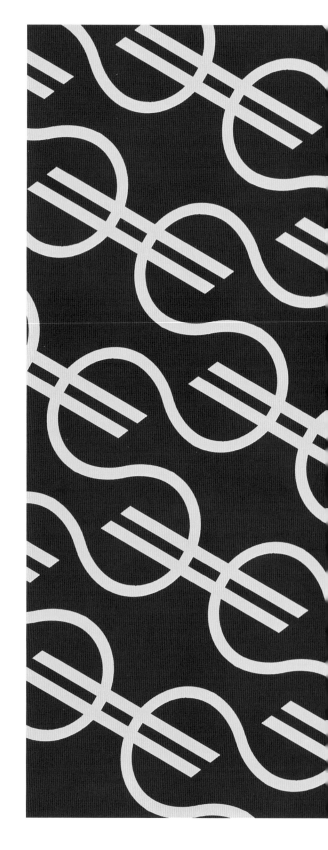

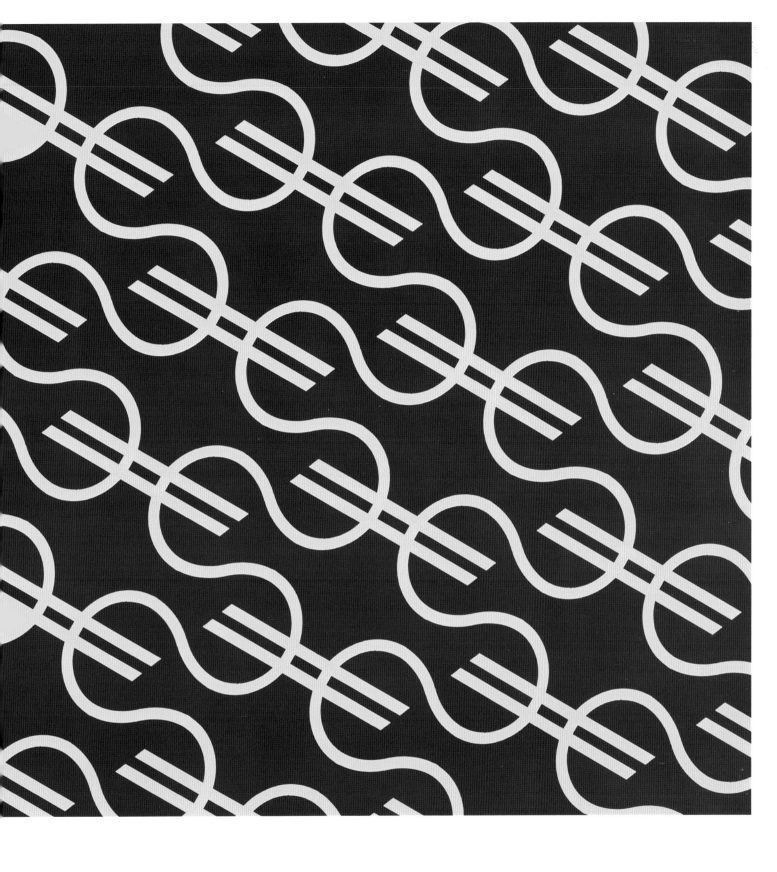

Watch Out!

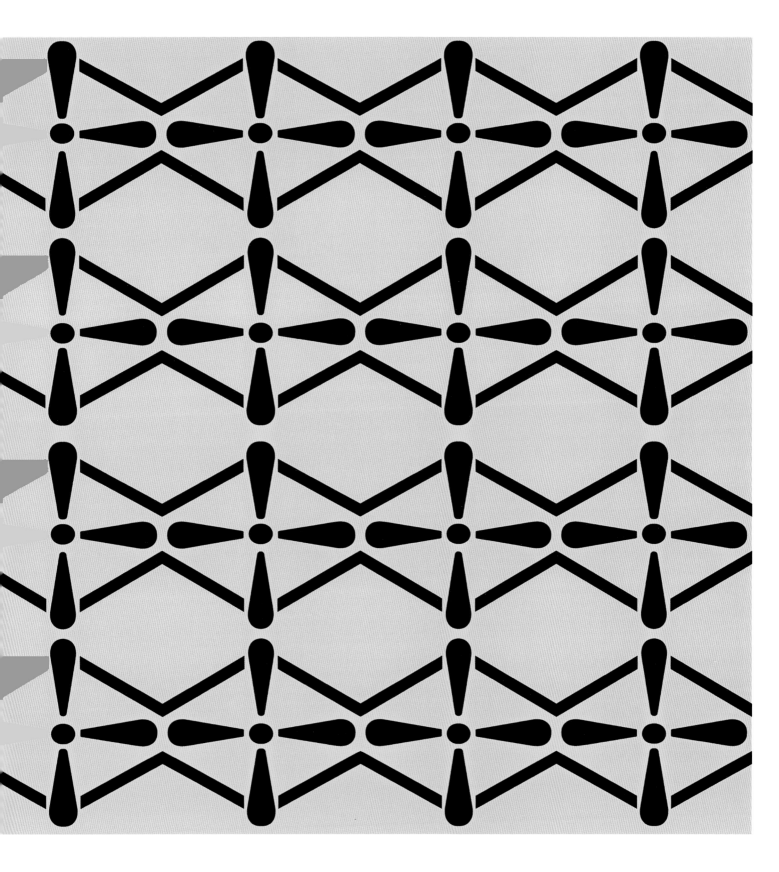

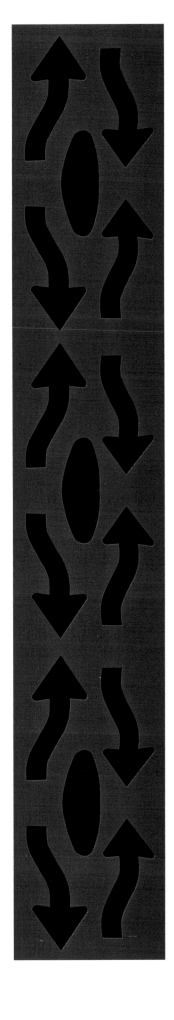

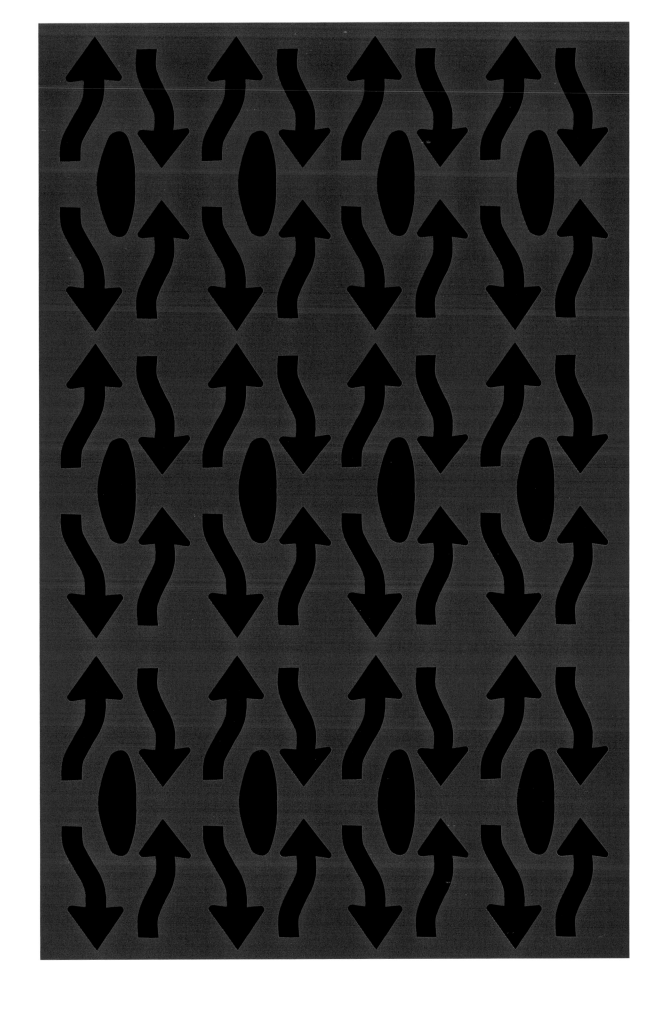

Road bends ahead

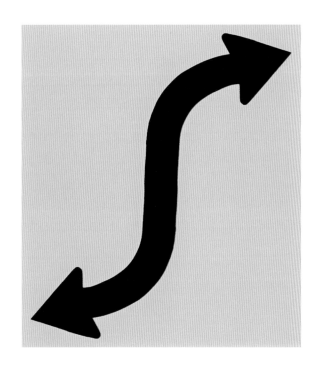

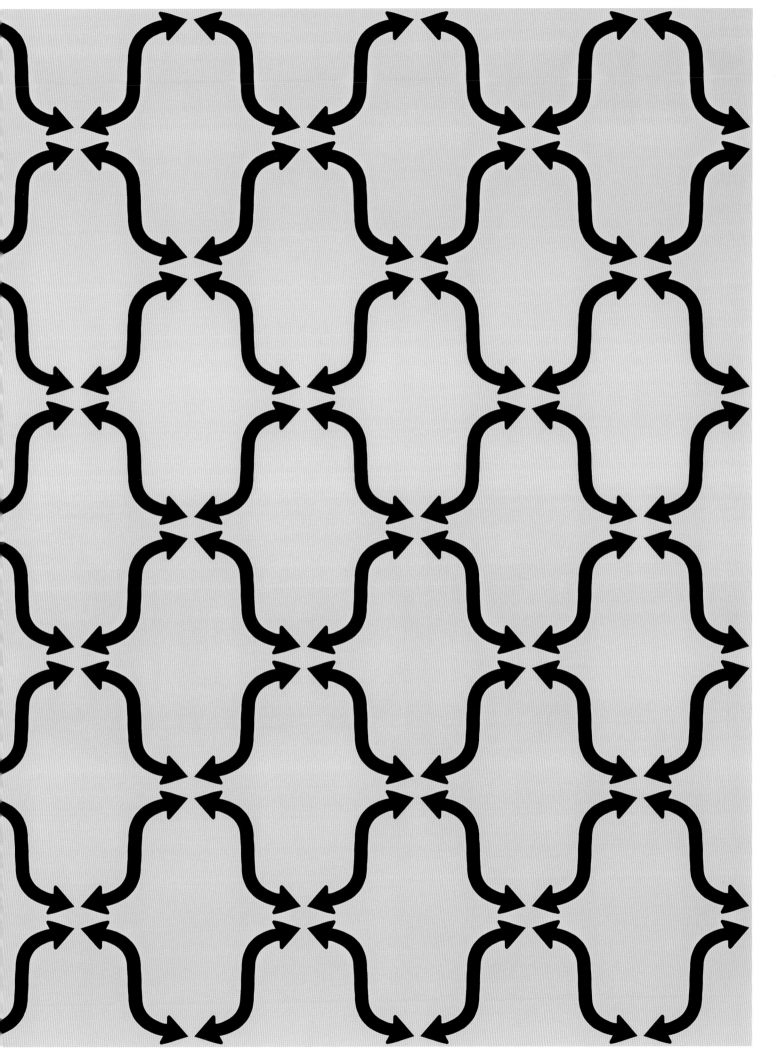

Diverging lanes

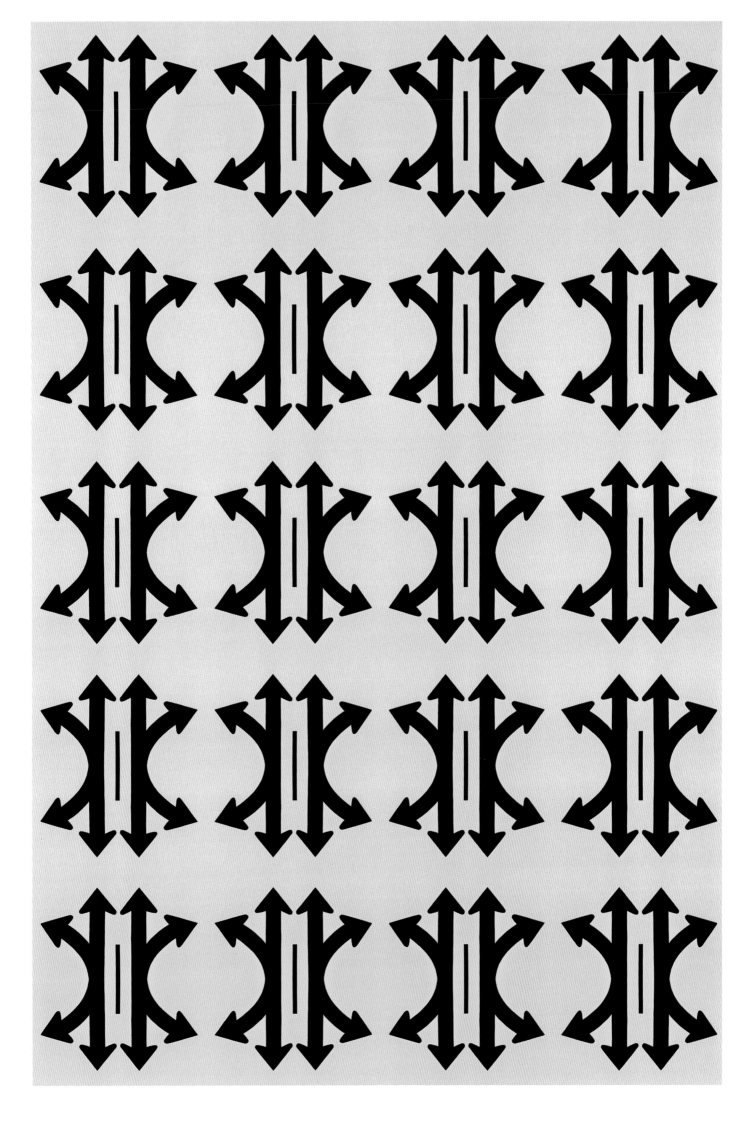

White arrows on blue (1)

White arrows on blue (2)

Road narrows

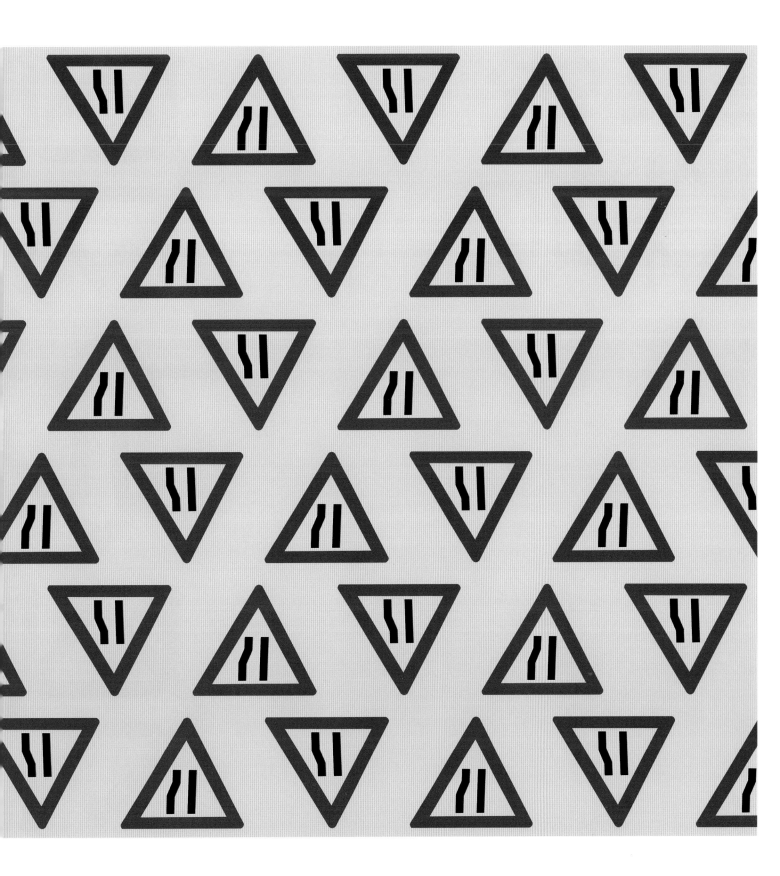

No right turn (1)

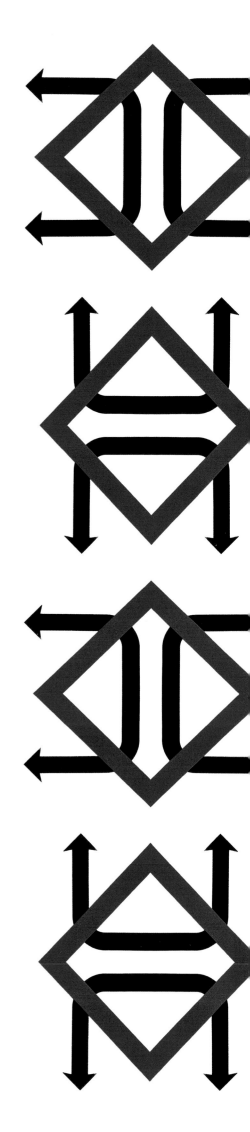

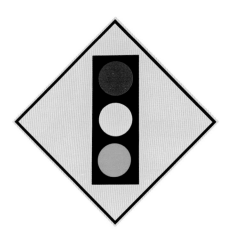

Traffic lights

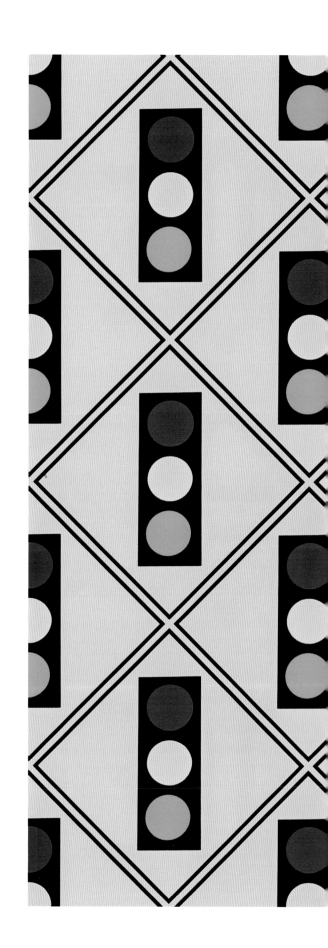

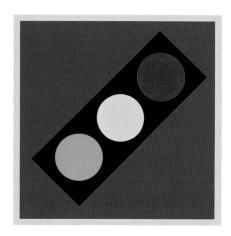

Traffic lights on blue

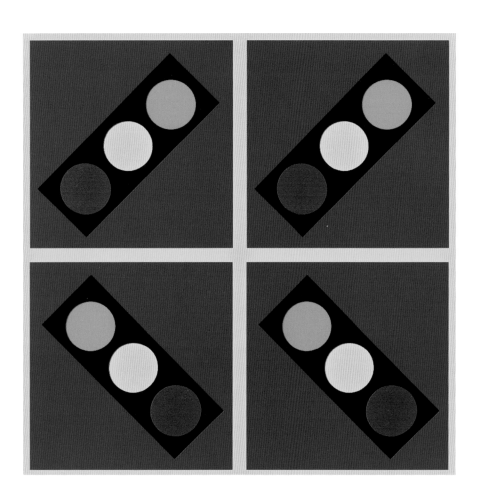

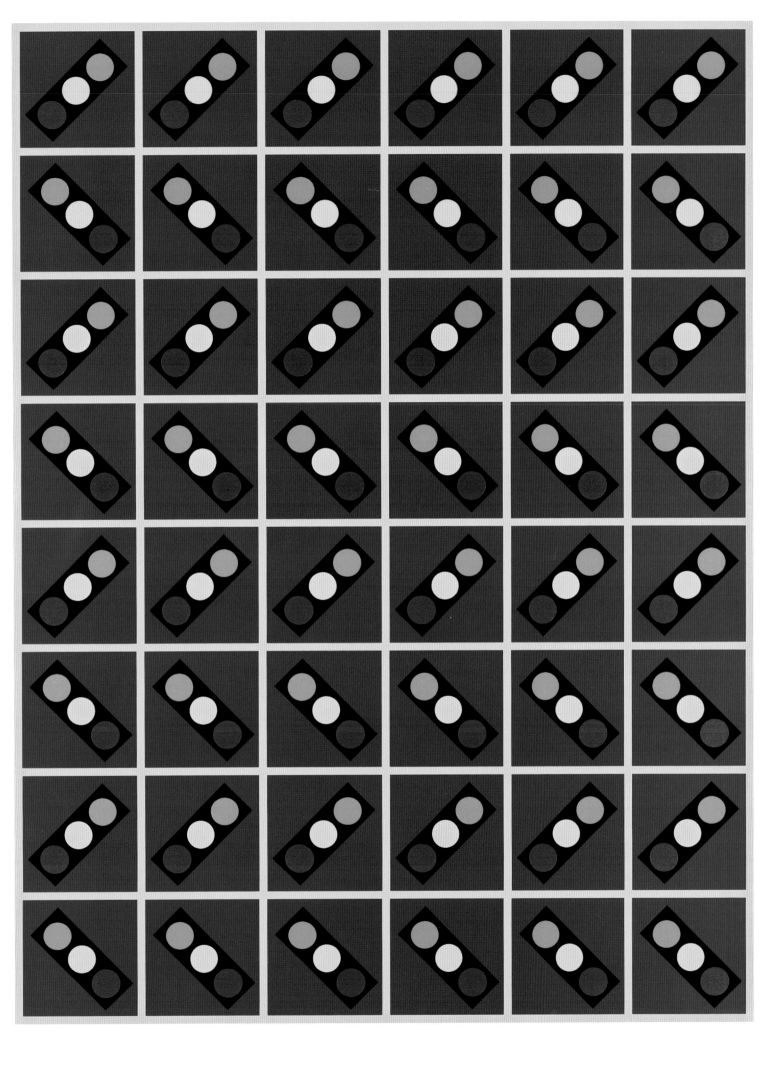

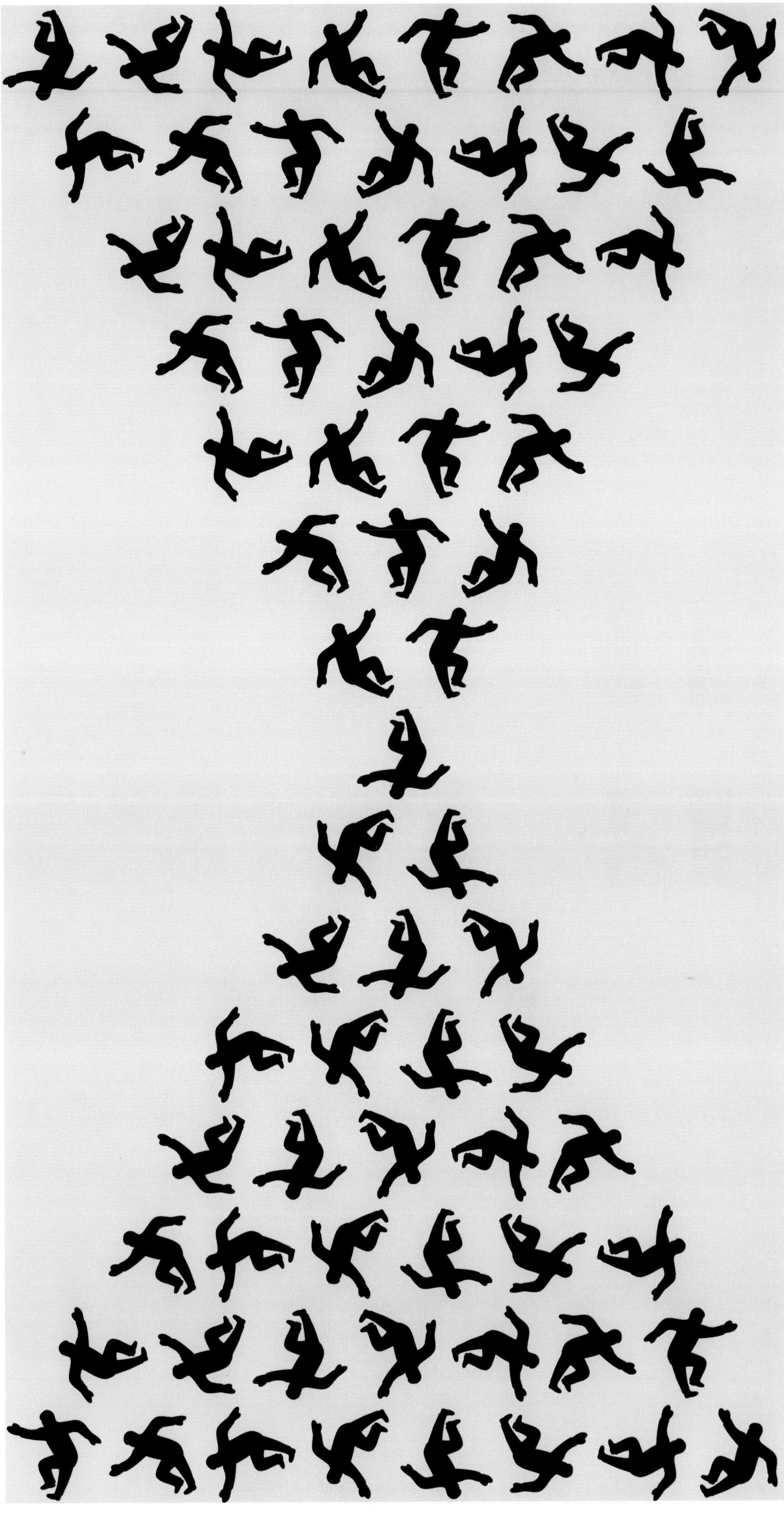

The Daily Round

Quo vadis?

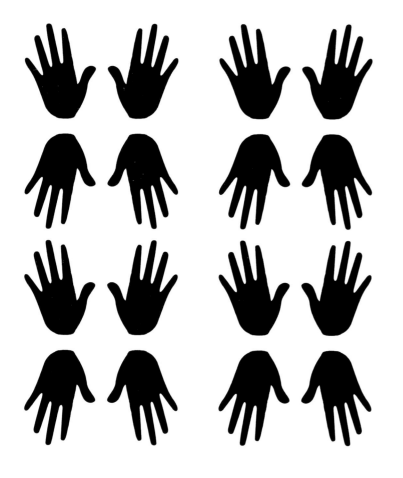

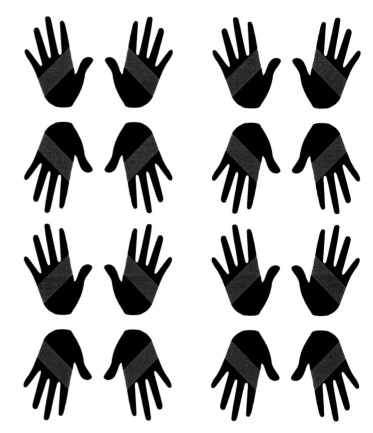

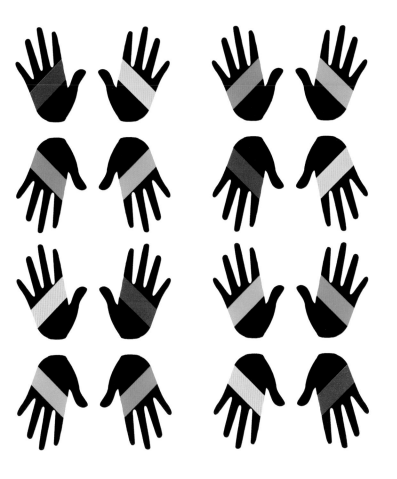

Rainbow nation

Black and white hands on red

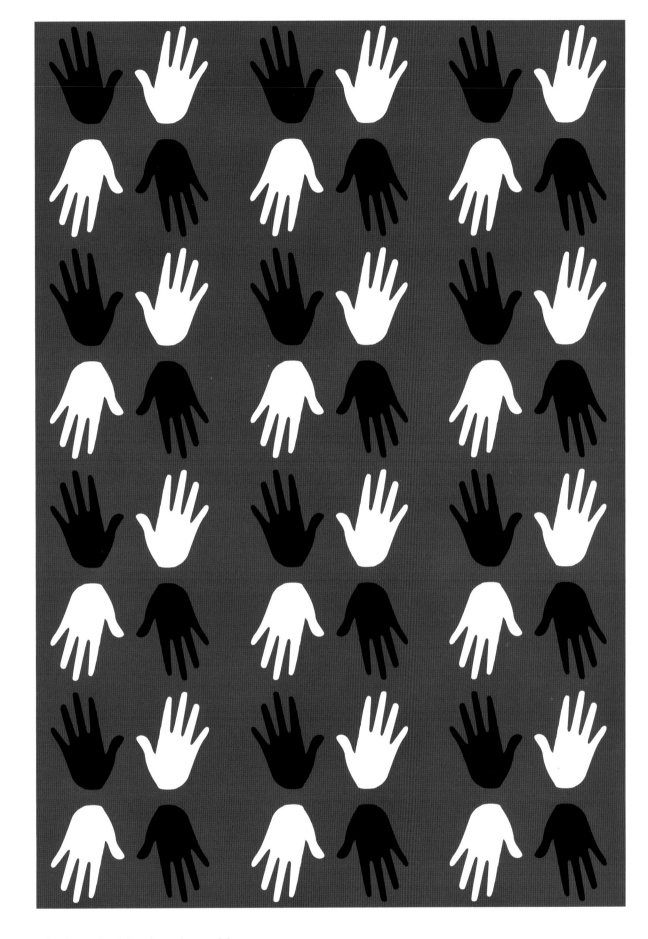

Black and white hands on blue

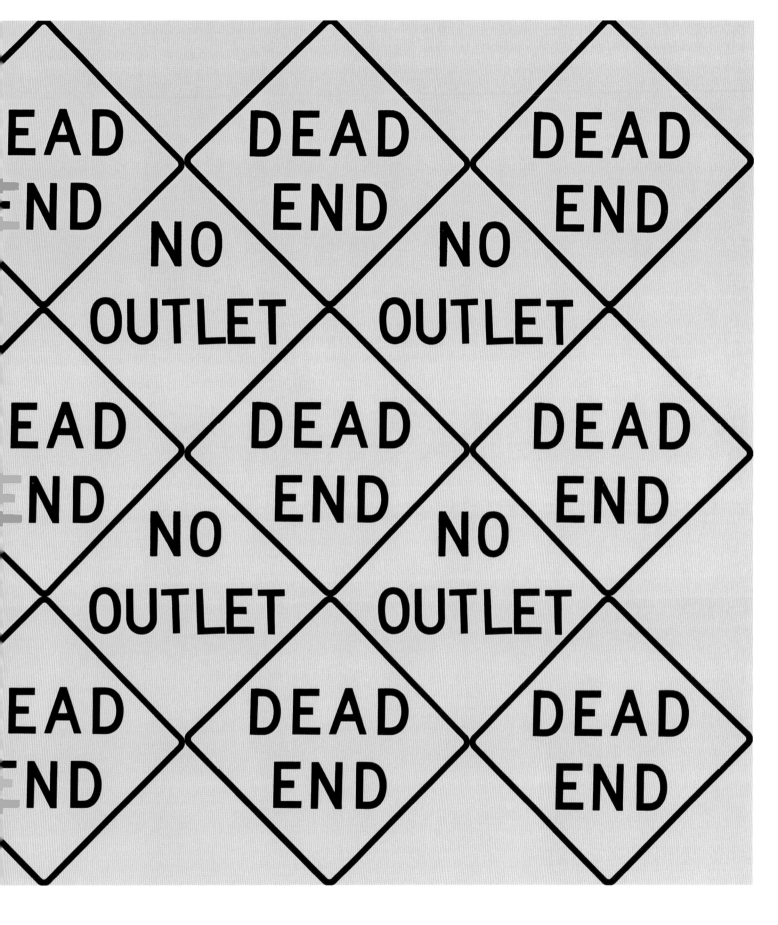

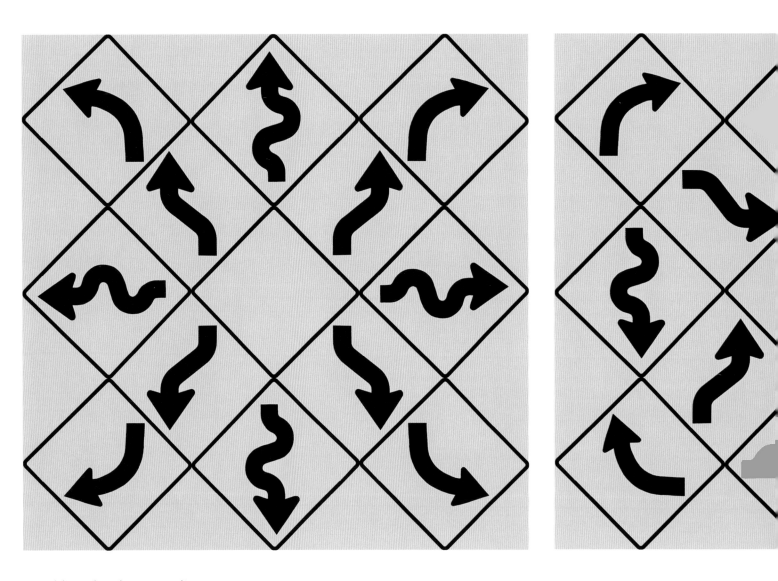

Road bends : three studies

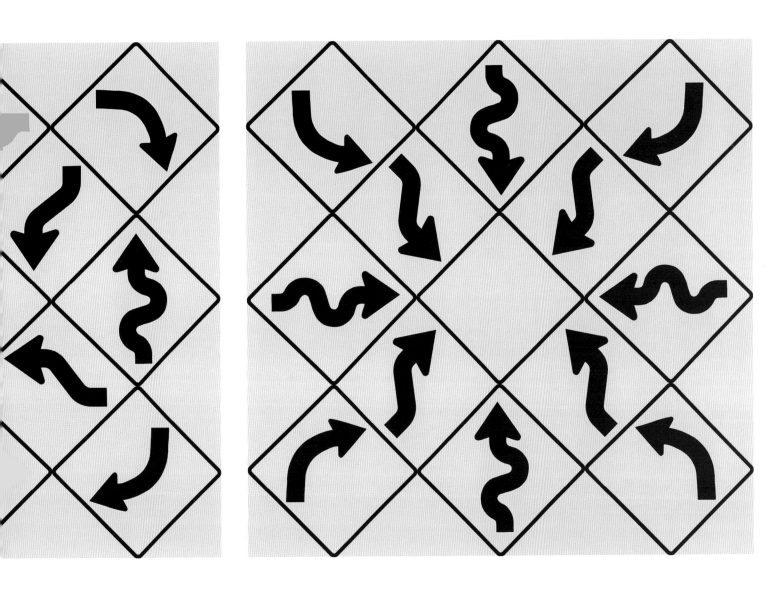

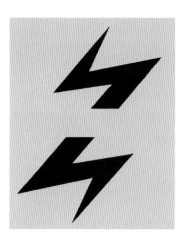

Red flash on yellow

Firehose reel (2)

No right turn (2)

Variations on a triangle (1)

Variations on a triangle (2)

Variations on a triangle (3)

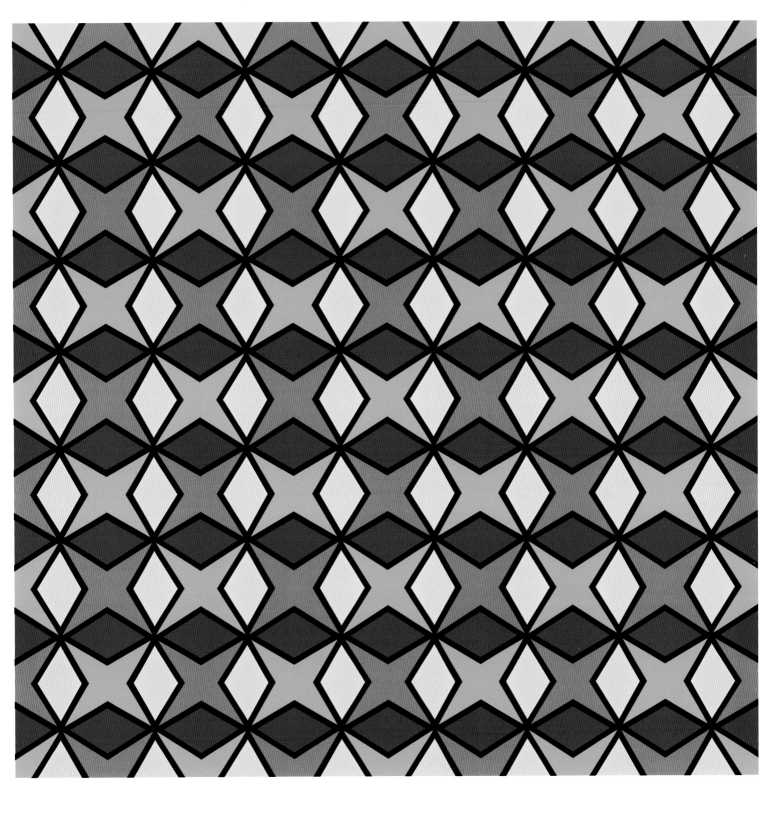

Variations on a triangle (4)

Road junction construct (1 and 2)

Road junction construct in four colors (1 and 2)